JP

Ezekiel

A PROPHET FOR ALL TIMES

CWR

Claire Musters

Contents

Introduction

Dramatic visions, unusual actions and a big focus on judgment makes Ezekiel one of the most bizarre – and probably least read – books of the Bible. At first glance it can seem almost impenetrable and totally irrelevant to us as modern-day readers, and yet within it there are deep truths about God, and His people, which are important for us to grasp. I encourage you to read the book of Ezekiel in full, as we'll be covering large chunks of Scripture each week.

My hope is that, as we unpack this somewhat foreboding and strange book, we will all truly understand the purpose of Ezekiel's prophecy, and the faithfulness of God to His people – throughout all of time.

Who was Ezekiel?
The book of Ezekiel was written around 571 BC and centres on the actions and messages of the prophet Ezekiel. He was the son of Buzi, a Zadokite priest, and was born and raised in Judah. He was preparing to be a priest in 597 BC when the Babylonians attacked and carried off 10,000 captives to exile in Babylon (see 2 Kings 24:10–14). Five or so years later, Ezekiel was called by God to become a prophet.

Ezekiel was called through a dramatic vision that completely undid him – he was never the same again. Such a big impact was necessary, as God was calling him to a life of absolute obedience that involved speaking God's Word to people who simply wouldn't listen.

Ezekiel was a young contemporary of the prophet Jeremiah, and while Jeremiah was in the city of Jerusalem prophesying that it would soon fall to the Babylonians, Ezekiel was conveying the exact same message to the exiled people. And yet both groups of people refused to believe that Jerusalem would ever fall – after all, it was

God's city, was it not? Surely He would protect it for all time? How wrong they were...

The history

One thousand years before Ezekiel, the 12 tribes of Israel had been split up – the ten northern tribes had been carried off to Assyria after they ignored God's warnings through the prophets Hosea and Amos. Ezekiel's message was for the two southern tribes of Judah – despite being told by those in the north what could happen, they ignored what the earlier prophets Isaiah, Micah, Jeremiah and Habakkuk said to them.

King Josiah had tried to reform the people when he discovered the book of the Law and realised how far they had drifted from God's way (see 2 Kings 22). But it didn't work as their hearts were too far from God. Following Josiah were kings who did 'evil in the eyes of the Lord' (2 Kings 23:32), and even when Josiah's son Jehoiakim arrived on the throne, he wasn't particularly concerned with the people's spiritual state. Although he wasn't as bad as some of his predecessors, he was still a puppet-king, as was the later king Zedekiah.

Judah was surrounded by the superpowers of Egypt and Babylon. God continued to warn the people that He could save them if they drew close to Him, but if they remained faithless He would remove His hand of protection from them. But the people of Judah ignored God and so Nebuchadnezzar, the king of Babylon, invaded and controlled the country for three years before leaving. After that, Judah was attacked by the Arameans, Moabites and Ammonites (see 2 Kings 24:1–3). By the time Ezekiel was on the scene, the city of Jerusalem was pretty much all that was left of Judah – but foreign countries were controlling it.

The Babylonians returned and besieged the city when King Jehoiachin was on the throne, eventually capturing it and taking away all of its treasures, as Isaiah had originally prophesied (see Isa. 39:5–7). At the time, the Babylonians removed 7,000 army officers and soldiers from Judah as well as about 1,000 skilled workers and artisans – 10,000 people in total (this was when Daniel was exiled to Babylon – see 2 Kings 24:8–17).

Judah's new king, Zedekiah (placed on the throne and given a new name by Nebuchadnezzar), was allowed to remain in Jerusalem with a small army. However, when he rebelled Nebuchadnezzar returned, eventually capturing the army, killing Zedekiah's children and gouging out his eyes before calling for Jerusalem to be destroyed (see 2 Kings 25).

A prophet is called

It was during the time of exile in Babylon (before the fall of Jerusalem) that God first called Ezekiel to be a prophet (we will discover more about how this happened in week one). Ezekiel's prophetic messages were often given through apocalyptic language, using dramatic visuals and symbolism. As we will see, God showed him what was happening in Jerusalem even though he was far away in Babylon. Through God, Ezekiel was also able to see into the future.

Ezekiel continued to fearlessly preach God's message to the exiled Jews on the streets of Babylon even when he was ignored. He spoke of God's judgments, firstly against His own people, and then to the surrounding nations. Ultimately, however, Ezekiel's message was one of hope, deliverance and blessing for those God calls His own. God is a Holy God, and He must uphold His name. But His heart, throughout the whole book, was to bring His people back to Himself. He never gave up on them – just as He never gives up on us. While our circumstances may be very different, Ezekiel has much to say to us too – he is certainly a prophet for all times.

WEEK ONE

Called and commissioned

Icebreaker

Can anyone remember a really vivid dream? Or has anyone ever seen a vision they are willing to share with the group?

Bible Readings

- Ezekiel 1–3
- Daniel 1; 7
- Jeremiah 1
- Revelation 1:12–18; 4:6–7

Opening Our Eyes

We learn right at the start of the book of Ezekiel that he was a priest – or about to become one. As verse one indicates, Ezekiel was 30 at the time, which was the usual age for a man to enter the priesthood. However, God had other ideas for him. Jerusalem was on the brink of collapse and most of its inhabitants had been exiled in Babylon. Their near ruin was due to their own unfaithfulness towards God, yet they didn't recognise this. God needed someone reliable that He could speak to the people through; Ezekiel was chosen.

Ezekiel's name means 'God strengthens', and, as we will see in the coming weeks, this was the overall message he was asked to convey – that, despite their great sin, God remained strong and would ultimately restore His people.

God called Ezekiel through an exceedingly vivid vision. In chapter 1, Ezekiel described how 'the hand of the LORD was on him' (v3) and 'the heavens were opened' (v1). In his vision, he witnessed a violent storm from the north, which many scholars believe was symbolic of the armies of Babylon, God's chosen means of judgment. In the centre of the surrounding brilliant light/fire were four incredible living creatures, each with four faces, which were a combination of animal, human and angel. Beside each creature was a wheel that could go in any direction, depending on whichever way the Spirit went. The wheels were all covered in eyes (v18), signifying that God can see everywhere. The fact that God is omnipresent was an important point for Ezekiel to grasp and pass on as, rather than being static, He was always with the people in Babylon (the Israelites believed God's dwelling was inside the temple in Jerusalem so may have felt He was no longer with them).

Above the creatures and wheels appeared 'the likeness of the glory of the LORD' (Ezek. 1:28). Ezekiel used lush language here, which is reminiscent of that in Revelation; no doubt he was trying to capture the essence of what he had seen – and yet words were simply not adequate. Ezekiel told us that on the throne was a 'figure like that of a man' (Ezek. 1:26). Just seeing God would be enough to change someone's life forever and yet He also then turned and spoke directly to Ezekiel! God commissioned him in a very precise way, explaining exactly why His message was needed – and then providing details of what it should be.

Absolute obedience was required, starting with the eating of the scroll Ezekiel was presented with next. Covered with 'words of lament and mourning and woe' (Ezek. 2:9) it would have been reasonable to expect the scroll to taste bitter, and yet it was 'sweet as honey' (Ezek. 3:3).

God knew that the Israelites had hardened hearts so He told Ezekiel He would make his forehead 'like the hardest stone, harder than flint' (Ezek. 3:9) in order for him to stand strong in the midst of opposition and obstinacy from the people. As Ezekiel was lifted up physically by God's Spirit, he began to feel deep bitterness and anger at the behaviour of the people. He then sat among them for seven days, which was the customary period of mourning for the dead (see Gen. 50:10; 1 Sam. 31:13; Job 2:13). He was mourning for their spiritual state. It was after this time that God spoke again, calling Ezekiel His watchman. He laid quite a responsibility on Ezekiel, but also revealed His glory to him again. Ezekiel's response was that he 'fell face down' (Ezek. 3:23). After this, God explained that He would only open Ezekiel's mouth when He had something for him to say.

Discussion Starters

1. What are some of the life situations that occur unexpectedly, which can make us feel like our lives haven't turned out as we had hoped? How do we respond?

_____

_____

_____

_____

_____

2. The throne in Ezekiel's vision is depicted as able to move. Find some other descriptions of the throne in the Old Testament to compare and contrast.

_____

_____

_____

_____

_____

3. Ezekiel's vision of 'a figure like that of a man' has many similarities with that found in Revelation 1:12–18. Study both passages together, commenting on these similarities and what they could mean.

_____

_____

_____

_____

_____

4. What is the significance of the rainbow radiance surrounding the figure that Ezekiel describes?

_____

_____

_____

_____

_____

5. In Revelation 10:8–10, John is also told to eat a scroll. Take a look at the passage and compare and contrast it with Ezekiel's experience.

_____

_____

_____

_____

_____

6. Look again at Ezekiel's response to God's calling. Where else can we read a similar response to the glory of God? How do you respond to it today?

_____

_____

_____

_____

7. Discuss the symbolism of the four creatures Ezekiel saw.

_____

_____

_____

_____

_____

8. Ezekiel's face was set like flint by God because he had to deliver a difficult message that God knew the people wouldn't respond well to. Do we need similar single-mindedness in our culture today? Why?

_____

_____

_____

_____

Personal Application

Reflecting on such an incredible vision reminds us of who the God we serve actually is. Just taking time out to pause and meditate on such truths is important, as it is so easy to live busy lives that are somewhat disconnected from God – the Israelites were certainly doing that! It is in God's Word that we find the truths vital for our souls. Just as Ezekiel ate the scroll God gave him and discovered it to be sweet, if we regularly take in portions of the Bible we will find it is a great treasure that helps us live out our lives well.

Ezekiel was given the responsibility of warning the people of the coming judgment. Today, we are all charged with taking God's good news to the world (Matt. 28:18). Do we take this responsibility as seriously as Ezekiel did?

Seeing Jesus in the Scriptures

When God spoke to Ezekiel He called him 'son of man' (Ezek. 3:1), a phrase He actually uses 83 times in the book (Ezekiel is referred to as this more often than his own name). Jesus called Himself the same thing in the Gospels (Matt. 17:12, Mark 10:45, Luke 9:22), and He was certainly the fulfillment of both Daniel's vision of the heavenly being (Dan. 7), and Ezekiel's example of a prophet who is faithful to serving God and speaking His words, even when it involves suffering. Like Jesus, Ezekiel also started his prophetic ministry at the age of 30, performing miracles and preaching. Jesus was prophet, priest and king – the ultimate Son of Man (see Mark 2:10, Heb. 7:11–28).

WEEK TWO

Visual representations of God's judgment

Icebreaker

Has anyone told you something you were inclined not to believe? How did they persuade you it was true?

Bible Readings

- Ezekiel 4–14
- 2 Corinthians 3:12–18

Opening Our Eyes

We are now entering what many view as the truly impenetrable part of Ezekiel. Chapters 4–24 are about God's judgment on Judah and the holy city, Jerusalem. Even though there are so many chapters on this, we will be taking only two weeks to look at them! But, while the subject matter may be rather depressing, the visual imagery is rich. And let's always bear in mind that God involved Ezekiel in such bizarre demonstrations because His heart was for His people to listen and turn back to Him.

Sadly, even when Jerusalem had been taken by the Babylonians and the skilled people exiled, many believed that the judgment both Jeremiah and Ezekiel spoke about was being exaggerated, because the city still stood. But they had watered down God's words for too long – He was about to show them visibly, through what He asked Ezekiel to do (and say), why they were exiled (showing judgment in order to reform).

In this next set of chapters in the book of Ezekiel, we read about some of the strange things that Ezekiel was instructed to do by God. They all pointed to the fact that Jerusalem was going to fall:

• In total silence, Ezekiel drew a picture of the city of Jerusalem on a piece of clay and then acted out it being sieged;

• He was asked to lie on his left side for 390 days to show how many years Israel had been disobeying God, then 40 days on his right for the 40 years Judah had been rebellious. He was not allowed to move, symbolising how they would be imprisoned. The small amount of food God told him to eat reflected the fact that food would be scarce during the time Jerusalem lay under siege;

- Ezekiel was told by God to shave his head and beard and burn piles of the hair in different places, keeping a few strands. This represented what would happen to the people in Jerusalem (see Ezek. 4:11–12). The saved strands represented those who would be the remnant, saved by God (although even a few of those are burned up (Ezek. 5:4).

In chapter 7, Ezekiel spoke about the total destruction of Jerusalem and in the next chapter we are told that God took him to see the detestable things the people in Jerusalem were doing. In chapter 10, Ezekiel watched as God's glory literally departed from the temple. God went on to highlight the wickedness of the leaders and told Ezekiel to prophesy against them. In chapter 12, Ezekiel was told to act out leaving the city – which the exiled people would recognise as they had done it themselves only six years previously. But he was actually acting out what would happen to Zedekiah – he would have to creep out of the city at dusk (Ezek. 12:12). This showed the people that they couldn't trust their king to save Jerusalem. Ezekiel is clearly told by God all the details of what would happen – Ezekiel 12:13 foretells of Zedekiah being unable to see. God condemned the false prophets (Ezek. 13:10–12), but also got Ezekiel to give people the chance to repent (Ezek. 14:7). Over and over in this book we read the phrase: 'Then you will know that I am the LORD' (Ezek. 14:8). While some may say God could never be as judgmental as He is described as being here, He is holy and also gives fair warning. No longer could He tolerate the wickedness of the people – and He used foreign kings as the instruments of judgment.

Discussion Starters

1. Think of other instances in the Bible where the Word of God was watered down by the people, or the smaller details ignored, with disastrous consequences.

_____

_____

_____

_____

_____

2. What did God hold the exiled people accountable for?

_____

_____

_____

_____

_____

3. What was the reason that Ezekiel asked to be excused from having to cook his food over human excrement?

_____

_____

_____

_____

_____

4. In Ezekiel 9, God told the man in the vision to mark all those who were faithful on their foreheads, so that they could be spared when everyone else was killed. What other instances of such instructions from God does it remind you of?

_____

_____

_____

_____

_____

5. In Ezekiel 11:13, Ezekiel asked God whether he would completely destroy everyone. Who else asked God a similar question in the Old Testament?

_____

_____

_____

_____

_____

6. Ezekiel 11–13 shows how God's judgment was particularly aimed at the leaders and false prophets. Why do you think that was the case?

_____

_____

_____

_____

_____

7. Look at Ezekiel 11:18–20 alongside Jeremiah 32:39 (also Ezek. 18:31 and Ezek. 36:26). What do you think God means by the phrase 'undivided heart'?

_____

_____

_____

_____

_____

8. Ezekiel 11:23 talks of the glory of God stopping at the mountain to the east. Scholars believe this to be the Mount of Olives. Looking at Luke 19 and Matthew 24, comment on the significance of the Mount of Olives in Jesus' story.

_____

_____

_____

_____

_____

Personal Application

We could easily look upon the Israelites and immediately condemn them. After all, they were God's people, set aside and looked after by Him, so how could they be so easily swayed? God had given them land, they had built a temple for Him – but now they were worshipping the gods of the surrounding nations and were being corrupted by their love of money. Are we so different though? Whenever we allow culture to influence us, whenever we put our security in anything other than God, we are opening ourselves up to idolatry. Philippians 4:6–8 talks about only allowing that which is pure and right into our minds. With social media and visual communications so widespread, do we take as much care as to what is being fed into our hearts and minds as we could? It all affects us.

Seeing Jesus in the Scriptures

There is a small passage of hope within the vision that Ezekiel sees in 11:14–25. It talks about God removing our hearts of stone and giving us a heart of flesh. This is only possible through the ultimate sacrifice of Jesus. We all deserve the punishment and judgment that Ezekiel describes in this portion of his book, and yet God doesn't pour it out onto us because He has already poured it onto His Son. How incredible! The passage in 2 Corinthians included in the Bible readings this week explains how different things are for us under the New Covenant – when Ezekiel, and others, saw God's glory they fell down as though dead, but now: 'we all, who with unveiled faces contemplate the Lord's glory, are being transformed into his image with ever-increasing glory, which comes from the Lord, who is the Spirit' (2 Cor. 3:18).

WEEK THREE

Parables and other stark messages

Icebreaker

Can anyone think of an instance of when obedience to God cost you a great deal? How did it make you feel at the time? Or what about a difficult word He asked you to convey – did you think about how to present it in a way that was palatable?

Bible Readings

- Ezekiel 15–24
- Genesis 19
- Isaiah 11:1–5
- Hosea

Opening Our Eyes

Ezekiel continued to bring God's message of judgment to the people in Babylon. In the Ezekiel chapters we will be looking at this week, he warned of Jerusalem's imminent destruction and used lots of parables – one which depicted Judah as a useless vine. Then Ezekiel spoke of a deserted baby girl who God rescued and brought to prominence, only for her to prostitute herself. This reflected how Israel was raised in status and given the Promised Land but then became proud, thinking it was down to themselves. The foreign gods and their detestable practices, which they ended up adopting for themselves, also turned their heads (Ezek. 16:19–25). When Ezekiel spoke of specific dalliances with countries, he was also referring to their religious practices and political alliances. The people were looking to others rather than God for their security, but God would use these 'lovers' to be His agents of judgment (Ezek. 16:35–42).

In chapter 17, the vine represents Israel and the first eagle Nebuchadnezzar, who King Zedekiah looked to for salvation by making a treaty with. But Zedekiah soon reneged on the deal and looked to Egypt, the second eagle, for assistance. God took covenant seriously, and here highlighted the fact that Zedekiah had not only broken covenant with God Himself but also with the Babylonian king.

Even with all these visual representations and vivid parables, the people still didn't get it. They may have realised that God's judgment was indeed looming, but they blamed their ancestors. The Ten Commandments talk about God punishing the second and third generation (see Exod. 20:5), but the people had misconstrued this to abdicate any personal responsibility. So God told Ezekiel to state clearly that if someone sinned, they would be punished. This is a shift from referring to the people as a whole towards highlighting individual responsibility.

In chapter 19, Ezekiel used lament to talk about a lioness and two cubs – the lioness represented Judah and the cubs were the two kings Jehoahaz (2 Kings 23:31–33) who was taken to Egypt and Jehoiakim (2 Kings 24:8–17) who was captured and taken to Babylon (although some commentators say this could have referred to Zedekiah who was about to be taken – 2 Kings 25:7).

Chapter 20 is a review of Israel's past history – with a glimpse of God's future plans. It ends with Ezekiel putting a complaint before God that the people aren't listening because he is using parables (v49)! Chapter 21 then gives a clear indication that God's judgment would come through Babylon. In chapter 23 Ezekiel compared the northern and southern kingdoms to two sisters, Oholah and Oholibah, who prostituted themselves. Verses 22–26 then foretold the last attack on Jerusalem that destroyed the city (see, 2 Kings 25, Jer. 52). When Ezekiel called Jerusalem a cooking pot in chapter 24, this was about three years on from his first messages so the remnant in Jerusalem probably felt they were safe as they weren't exiled. But Ezekiel proclaimed this message to the exiles on the very day that the Babylonians attacked the city (see v2).

Even though everything God asked Ezekiel to do seems extreme, probably the hardest aspect to understand can be found in Ezekiel 24:15–27. Here God warned him that his wife was going to die, but told him he was not allowed to mourn as his response would be a picture of what would happen with the people. He again stated that He would take away their pride and joy, the temple in Jerusalem, and yet outward signs of grief would not be enough to express the deep shock and pain they would feel when that happened.

Discussion Starters

1. Look at Isaiah 5:1–7 and discuss both Ezekiel and Isaiah's descriptions of Israel as a vine. Why did God need to prune the nation?

2. Take a close look at Ezekiel 16 and then discuss what the vivid imagery reveals about God's care for His people – and their ingratitude.

3. In the latter part of chapter 16, Judah is compared to Sodom. Look at Genesis 19:1–29 and discuss what Sodom's sin was.

4. As we have seen, Ezekiel used a lot of parables to convey God's message. Jesus used parables too – take a look at some together and see how they brought His messages to life.

5. Ezekiel 18 is a very clear portrayal of personal responsibility. Spend some time reflecting on how Jesus has taken away this burden – but also our continued responsibility in how we live in the light of His gift to us.

_____

_____

_____

_____

_____

6. A lament is an expression of grief or sorrow. Take a look at some other biblical laments and discuss how effective they are at conveying their messages.

_____

_____

_____

_____

7. Hosea was another man whose personal life was used as a mirror, revealing more about God's relationship with Israel. Discuss the extremity of God's request and Hosea's obedience.

_____

_____

_____

_____

8. Re-read Ezekiel 24:25–27. The destruction of the temple seems to be a turning point in Ezekiel's own life – why do you think that is?

_____

_____

_____

23

Personal Application

In the Ezekiel chapters we're studying this week, we see Ezekiel continuing to convey God's message to His people with such obedience, even in the face of huge personal cost. It is here too that we first read about the importance of individual, rather than corporate, holiness. It is interesting to think about how God referred to the temple in Jerusalem as the people's 'stronghold, their joy and glory, the delight of their eyes' (Ezek. 24:25 – see also v21). While we may not trust in a city or temple, what do we take pride in? Has anything else taken the place of God in our hearts? Think about what things you would refer to as your pride and joy – your family? What about friendships, your job or even your ministry? Although we can view the more vivid chapters in this section as quite disturbing and grotesque, anything that we put our trust or pride in more than God may have become an idol in our lives. That's a sobering thought…

Seeing Jesus in the Scriptures

What is interesting is that, even in the midst of a huge tirade of preaching on judgment, God Himself declares (in Ezek. 17:22–24) another hint of hope. In this section, He looks forward to Jesus, describing a splendid cedar tree that He will raise up as a place of safety and shelter. God is revealing that this, our method of salvation, comes from Him – it is all His doing. As Isaiah 11 states, Jesus is that tender shoot that *will* bear fruit. Ultimately He is the only one we can truly trust in, so we need to ensure we stay attached to Him.

WEEK FOUR

Surrounding nations

Icebreaker

Using an online biblical map or Bible atlas, take turns until you have located all the nations mentioned in these chapters so that you can see how they relate geographically to Israel.

Bible Readings

- Ezekiel 25–32
- Revelation 18
- Amos 1–3

Opening Our Eyes

This week we will look closely at the middle part of
Ezekiel, which concentrates on God's judgment against
the surrounding nations who took advantage of the fall of
Jerusalem. Ezekiel spoke of the fall as having happened,
and yet the news hadn't officially reached the exiles. But
our attention is being focused on God's judgment on the
surrounding nations. Remember, Ezekiel wasn't simply being
patriotic – God only allowed him to speak when He had a
message He wanted him to share (Ezek. 3:25–27). Nations
such as the Edomites and Ammonites took horrendous
advantage of the people once Jerusalem had fallen, and
so God was distributing His justice on those who had
exploited His people.

The Old Testament prophets concentrated their messages
on God's people, but they also looked at the surrounding
nations – often to declare God's sovereignty over the world.

Interestingly, much of Ezekiel's prophetic utterances about
what would happen to the surrounding nations have
come true. In chapters 26 and 27, he talked about what
would happen to Tyre, the capital of Phoenicia, which
was located just north of Israel. Tyre and Judah had spent
years competing for trade, with Tyre dominating the sea
trade routes and Judah the land ones. When Judah was
defeated, Tyre thought it had all the trade sewn up but
after the fall of Jerusalem, Nebuchadnezzar then laid
siege to Tyre. However, when Ezekiel predicted that the
whole city would be thrown into the sea and it's location
a place fishermen where would spread out their nets
(Ezek. 26:12–13), he was describing what would happen
in the time of Alexander the Great. When the ancient
Greek king marched towards Egypt with his army, the
inhabitants of Tyre utilised their many fishing boats and
rowed out to supposed safety on their island settlement.
But Alexander the Great responded by throwing every

part of the city into the sea and creating a huge bridge out towards the island, which he then travelled across to defeat Tyre in 332 BC. The modern city of Tyre is still made out of the island and the old site is a pile of rock and rubble, used for spreading fishing nets across.

Rather than using parables or allegorical language, most of this section is straightforward. Tellingly, while Ezekiel worked in a clockwise direction when dealing with all the surrounding nations, he missed Babylon out. Scholars have come up with various reasons for this: perhaps now the exiles were in Babylon they couldn't speak of it directly – although what seems most likely is that Babylon was viewed differently as God Himself indicated it was the instrument of punishment against Israel.

While most of what Ezekiel said was about nations, one man was singled out – the king of Tyre. An example of supreme pride, he said: 'I am a god' (Ezek. 28:1). Many scholars believe that, while this was talking about a specific person, it also has a wider application – Satan's pride. In chapter 29, we see that the Egyptian Pharaoh did something similar, saying he had made the Nile (Ezek. 29:3).

Egypt, and its Pharaoh, is mentioned in four chapters. Judah's existence had been hugely tied up with this country. In Ezekiel 29:6, Egypt is criticised for not coming to her rescue when she asked for help.

In Ezekiel 28:25–26 we see a glimpse of God's saving hand. The phrase 'then they will know that I am the Lord their God', which is repeated throughout the book, appears in two forms – one showing that the surrounding nations would recognise Him as the one true God, and another that His own people would too.

Discussion Starters

1. Look at Amos 1–3 together. What similarities – and what differences – can you pick out between those chapters and the ones in Ezekiel?

_____

_____

_____

_____

2. Discuss together what the main reasons for God's judgment against each neighbouring country was.

_____

_____

_____

_____

3. The language used in these chapters seems quite harsh, which is understandable as God speaks of judgment. Look at Psalm 137 and discuss some of the phrases used there. How does reading Ezekiel help to understand the violent language?

_____

_____

_____

_____

4. Compare and contrast what is said about Tyre in Ezekiel 26–27 with what is said about Babylon in Revelation 18.

_____

_____

_____

_____

5. Daniel is mentioned in Ezekiel 28. Already known as a wise person throughout Nebuchadnezzar's kingdom, what was different about him?

_____

_____

_____

_____

_____

6. Pharaoh is likened to a great monster (Ezek. 29:3). The Hebrew word *tannin* means 'sea monster'. This word also appears in Isaiah 27:1 and Amos 9:3. Look these up and discuss the context.

_____

_____

_____

_____

7. Referring to Egypt as a cedar tree is an oft-used image. Look up some of the others in Ezekiel itself (see Ezekiel 19:10–14; 26:19–21; 28:11–19). Discuss why you think it is a useful image.

_____

_____

_____

_____

8. Discuss how our culture often belittles God and His people. How can we approach talking to people who believe there are many paths to God?

_____

_____

_____

_____

Personal Application

God does not tolerate human pride, the ultimate example of which is a human setting themselves up as a god. Adam and Eve fell for the lure of ultimate knowledge dangled in front of them by the serpent. They gave in to pride, as they wanted to have the same level of knowledge as God. How easily are we lured by the things around us and the promises our culture makes to us? In a world where many set themselves up as their own gods, feeling they are the only person they need to answer to, we need to be careful not to allow that embracing of pride to affect us too.

Seeing Jesus in the Scriptures

It is interesting to note that Jesus spoke of Tyre in Matthew 11:22 – referring to it as a city worthy of God's judgment as it was known as one full of wickedness. But in this context, He was saying it would be more bearable for Tyre on the day of judgment then it for would be the other towns He visited that did not recognise Him.

In Ezekiel 29:21 it says, 'On that day I will make a horn grow for the Israelites'. The horn was often a symbol of strength. Some scholars point out its similarity to Psalm 132:17: 'I will make a horn grow for David'. In this instance, while it is referring to a descendant, it is also looking right the way through to Jesus, with the verse talking about 'my anointed one'. So there could be a messianic element to the horn reference in Ezekiel too. One thing is for certain, the people needed rescuing as they could not save themselves.

WEEK FIVE

A renewal of God's promises

Icebreaker

Has anyone received a promise from God that they've had to hold on to for a long time? How did they do that practically?

Bible Readings

- Ezekiel 33–37
- Philippians 2:1–11
- Titus 3:4–6

Opening Our Eyes

The next chapters explore another new direction in Ezekiel's prophecies, this time turning back to Judah and God's promise of restoration. In Ezekiel 33, God reminded Ezekiel that he was God's watchman, there to bring God's warning in order to turn the people from wickedness.

In Ezekiel 33:21, a messenger from Jerusalem arrived and told Ezekiel that all that he had warned would happen had in fact taken place. This vindicated Ezekiel as it showed he had spoken the truth and, as God had released his mouth, he was free to speak at will. The people were drawn to hear his message, and yet they still did not act on it – they continued to be a rebellious people. Part of this was down to bad leadership – God criticised the bad shepherds and said that He Himself would be the shepherd tending for the lost, binding up the injured etc. And in Ezekiel 34, He reminds them of His intention to make 'a covenant of peace' (v25).

After this, and a prophecy against Edom, the new message on Ezekiel's lips was of restoration. God pointed out that it was for His name, rather than their behaviour, that He would save His people.

We now come to the most cited chapter in Ezekiel 37 – the valley of dry bones. This was an incredibly vivid vision; Ezekiel was literally transported to the valley. As a Jew, particularly one who had trained to be a priest, he would have felt defiled as soon as he went near the dead, and yet God called him to walk up and down among them. This reflected exactly what Ezekiel had been doing throughout his adult life – walking among the spiritually dead, speaking God's words to them. It is also a wonderful picture of what God does for each one of us: breathing life into our spiritually dead state through Jesus.

In this chapter, the valley represented the trouble the people had got into. It also looked forward to what God was going to do for the whole nation: raise them up as a whole, living, breathing army, full of vitality and ready to take possession of everything He had for them. It must have seemed quite ridiculous to Ezekiel to be asked to prophesy over dead bones, but he continued to be obedient – presumably by now familiar with God's strange requests!

This chapter ends with another physical sign, which Ezekiel was asked to act out. He obediently took two sticks of wood (representing the north and south tribes) and placed them as one, a sign of unity and being under God's leadership. Historically this did not happen, but it can also be seen as a prophetic sign of God uniting Jews and Gentiles together. As Jesus alludes to in John 10:16 and Paul explains in Ephesians 3:4–6, the gospel message is that Gentiles are heirs alongside Israel.

As we can see, there are various levels at which these chapters in Ezekiel can be read – like so many other Old Testament prophecies there was a partial fulfilling when the exiled Jews were allowed back to Jerusalem and experienced something of a spiritual renewal (see the books of Ezra and Nehemiah). The prophecy of renewal also came to pass at Pentecost, when the Holy Spirit descended on thousands (see Acts 2). The world has seen other moments of revival, but of course the ultimate fulfillment will be when Jesus returns and God brings all things together (see Rev. 21).

Discussion Starters

1. Can you think of other biblical examples in which God's message is clear and the people seem to be listening but they don't act on it?

_____

_____

_____

_____

_____

2. Look at the description of shepherds (and God as shepherd) in Ezekiel 34 and compare it with David's (1 Sam. 16:1–13; 17:34) as well as Jesus' (Isa. 40:11, John 10:1–18, Luke 15:1–7). What are the characteristics of good and bad shepherds?

_____

_____

_____

_____

_____

3. Take some time to meditate together on Psalm 23. What does God, our true shepherd, provide for us?

_____

_____

_____

_____

_____

4. In Ezekiel 34 and 36 the imagery of trees, branches and fruit occurs again, this time positively. What was this symbolic of?

_____

_____

_____

_____

5. In Ezekiel 36, we begin to see details of what God's new covenant will be like with His people. Compare and contrast the old and new covenants.

_____

_____

_____

_____

_____

6. The transformation in the valley of the dry bones only happens once Ezekiel has prophesied as instructed. Do you think we listen to prophetic voices in our time? Why or why not?

_____

_____

_____

_____

_____

7. Read Ezekiel 37 alongside Jeremiah 31. How do they help flesh out the story of each other?

_____

_____

_____

_____

_____

8. How can Ezekiel 37:14 be viewed as a promise to churches that may find themselves in difficulty, or simply not in the place they would like to be?

_____

_____

_____

_____

Personal Application

Although the chapters in Ezekiel read this week reveal God's mercy towards an unfaithful people, and we know that our salvation is because of Jesus rather than anything we've done, we do still bear some responsibility for walking in holiness day by day. With this in mind, why not ask God to show you if there are any areas of your life today that you have allowed to be shaped by the culture around you rather than by His Word. He also holds us accountable in whatever area of leadership we may have, so it is important to check our motives regularly – do we enjoy the status of leadership or do we seek the welfare of others before ourselves?

Seeing Jesus in the Scriptures

We have already seen that Jesus is the true shepherd. He certainly laid down His life for us. When God talked about giving His people a heart of flesh rather than stone, that necessitated a huge change, one that preachers often liken to surgery. But, as we saw with the people of Israel, often their transformation didn't last. Thank God that when Jesus paid the ultimate sacrifice (see Heb. 13:20–21), He provided the way for the eternal covenant of peace to be brought to fruition (see Titus 3:4–6). He also ensured that we will escape that final terrifying act of judgment from God. When Jesus spoke to Nicodemus, He revealed to him the need for a complete cleansing by God through the Holy Spirit (see John 3). We need to allow Jesus to have full access to our hearts and minds daily.

WEEK SIX

God's triumph over evil

Icebreaker

Ask for volunteers to give a potted history of the people of Israel from the Old Testament, and how God intervened in their salvation, in under one minute.

Bible Readings

- Ezekiel 38–39
- Romans 9–11
- Revelation 20

Opening Our Eyes

The two chapters in Ezekiel that we are looking at this week are known as 'apocalyptic' and seem to interrupt the flow of the book, which up until now was seemingly working towards the climax of Israel's restoration. Instead, chapters 38 and 39 pause in order to talk about how God is going to bring a great victory to the people against all those around them.

The prophecy is specifically set against a man named Gog, from the land of Magog. Commentators aren't entirely sure about who this could be, but the Bible does mention Gog and Magog in two other places. Firstly, in Genesis 10:1–3 there is a person called Magog mentioned in Noah's lineage, while in Revelation 20:7–10, Gog and Magog are symbolic of those who oppose God. Some scholars have said that the Gog that Ezekiel referred to in Chapter 38 was Gyges, the king of Lydia, while others believe it to be the later king Alexander the Great, but, whether symbolic or a literal person, this figure can nevertheless be seen as a representation of the military forces that opposed God. As Ezekiel never saw the actual conflict (which he was told to prophecy would come from the north) take place and there isn't a clear indication of it occurring in history since his time, perhaps this could even be a battle that is yet to come.

The battle that is described shows Gog invading from the north (alongside other nations – see Ezek. 38:5–6) to destroy God's people, who are by this time settled in their land peacefully. But God is actually orchestrating events (verses 16–17 indicate He brings them against Israel) and will rise up to vindicate both His holy name and His people, completely destroying the invaders. He states that the weapons the invaders brought with them would be used as firewood by the Israelites for seven years afterwards (see Ezek. 39:9–10).

In Ezekiel 38:4, God says He will put hooks in the invaders' jaws, which may be a reference back to the big sea monster we looked at in chapter 29. As this imagery is more akin to a mythical creature, it could back up the interpretation of Gog being a personification of all evil people in the world.

These two chapters continually use a phrase from God: 'I will'. This is a covenant phrase that He uses throughout the Old Testament, but here the examples are about what He will do to those nations set against His people, how He will return His wayward nation to a land of safety and how He will be proved holy and above all other gods.

It is important to understand that Hebrew poetry and semi-poetical writing often used repetition, expanding on details as it did so. Ezekiel 39 is therefore not full of contradictions to the previous chapter (as some commentators have read it); rather it builds on what is said in Ezekiel 38, providing a fuller picture of how God is going to destroy the invaders.

In Ezekiel 39:17–20 there is a rather gruesome description of God calling His people to feast on the sacrifice He has prepared for them, which included horses and riders.

Towards the end of Ezekiel 39:26, God mentions how His people seem to forget Him and become unfaithful when they live in safety. It is His wonderful mercy and His commitment to the promises made in His covenant that motivate Him to continue to rescue them (and us). How easy is it, when we are comfortable, to take His love and care for granted?

Discussion Starters

1. Compare and contrast the description of the battle prophesised in these two Ezekiel chapters with the one mentioned in Revelation 20.

2. Look at some of the 'I will' verses we have read this week and discuss what they reveal about God and His actions.

3. There are other prophets who spoke of a huge battle between the forces of evil and the people of God. Can you think of some examples of prophets who used similar language to Ezekiel?

4. Throughout the Bible we see God's people become restless and unfaithful whenever they settle in safety. Why do you think that is?

5. What hope can we draw from the description of God rising up to battle for His people?

_____

_____

_____

_____

_____

6. The idea of God's feast is also seen in Zephaniah 1:7–9, while Revelation 19:17–21 includes similar imagery of gorging on flesh. Why do you think the description is so vivid – and grotesque to us today?

_____

_____

_____

_____

_____

7. Look up some descriptions of God's people being persecuted. How did they continue to glorify Him in the midst of suffering?

_____

_____

_____

_____

_____

8. God's people have felt deep opposition throughout the centuries. Take some time to discuss how the Church is being persecuted today, and what you can do?

_____

_____

_____

_____

_____

Personal Application

God's purpose in these chapters was to vindicate His holy name and bring His people to Himself. This is something that He continues to do, and will, ultimately, do for one final time before the day of judgment. This is a truth that we can cling to when we are feeling pressure from those around us to conform. We may not face physical persecution, as many around the world today do, but often our culture tries to fit us into its mould. However, as *The Message* version of Romans 12:1–2 says: 'Don't become so well-adjusted to your culture that you fit into it without even thinking. Instead, fix your attention on God… Unlike the culture around you, always dragging you down to its level of immaturity, God brings the best out of you, develops well-formed maturity in you.'

Seeing Jesus in the Scriptures

This apocalyptic section in Ezekiel does not directly reference Jesus as other chapters have (with their messianic hints), but there is imagery similar to Revelation in places. As the chapters describe what some see as a final battle that has yet to be seen, and culminate in God having compassion on His people and pouring His Spirit on them, it reminds us that this is all only possible through Jesus, the sacrificial lamb of God. He is the only one that is deemed worthy, as Revelation 5 states. Let us join with all the creatures on heaven and earth saying: 'Worthy is the Lamb, who was slain, to receive power and wealth and wisdom and strength and honour and glory and praise!' (Rev. 5:12).

WEEK SEVEN

A vision of restoration

Icebreaker

Has anyone undertaken a restoration project or witnessed a building being restored? As a group, think about the methods employed and discuss how much work goes into restoring something.

Bible Readings

- Ezekiel 40–48
- Revelation 21–22

Opening Our Eyes

Ezekiel 40 begins with a specific date, within the 25th year of the people's exile. Ezekiel was taken up to the top of a high mountain in order to see the most spectacular view – a vision of the splendid dwelling place that God intended for His people. Filled with descriptions of the temple court, from its outer courts right down to rooms for sacrifices and priests, all the precise measurements were given (Ezekiel certainly took note of the details!). It is absolutely enormous – one commentator worked out it would have been the size of 13 English cathedrals!

As we saw in week three, the people were really shaken when the temple in Jerusalem was destroyed. They had always thought that God would never let that happen – and many assumed He had left them when it was demolished. But that was not the case, and this splendid description of a temple serves as a reminder that He still intends to be with them.

In Ezekiel 8–10 we saw that God's glory had departed from the temple (and the reasons why), but in chapter 43 (19 years later) there was a new temple with worship restored to its proper place. God's glory once more descended and dwelt within the temple.

In the next few chapters of Ezekiel, God gives details of how the priesthood would be restored and daily worship and sacrifices resumed, as well as festivals celebrated. Interestingly, rather than a chief priest, chapter 44 mentions a prince (see verse 3 – some commentators say this could be anticipating the coming of Jesus, while others believe it can't be because the prince offers sacrifices – see Ezek. 46:4).

It appears that Ezekiel's exact temple was never built. It can be confusing as to why this might be, considering the amount of detail provided. Some say it was never intended to be a literal building – that it was purely a prophetic vision of hope for the people. Others say it must be a description of a heavenly temple and point to passages such as Hebrews 8:2; 9:11 to back this up. Still others believe that it was supposed to have been built but the leaders ignored God's instructions and only did what they could easily afford. There is a train of thought that says it is a description of a temple to be built in the future – however, the New Testament does make it clear that God no longer lives in manmade temples (see Acts 7:48; 17:24). We may not know the answer as to whether it will be constructed or not, but it does provide an incredible vision of God's majesty, glory and holiness.

In Ezekiel 45 we see the whole land being divided between the tribes. Allocated in horizontal strips from east to west, room was given to foreigners living with them (see Ezek. 47:22), showing that God accepts anyone who acknowledges who He is.

The 'river of God' is another passage from Ezekiel that is a favourite with preachers, probably because it talks of bringing life. Interestingly, the new river flowed from the south side of the temple, which was from the place of sacrifice. It travelled through into the Dead Sea, with the river giving new life so that fish would swim in it and trees flourished either side. This is symbolic of the life-giving nature of God's water, which can provide fresh life to even the most desolate of places. It is a description given to fill the people with hope.

Finally, Ezekiel's last chapter sees the city gates being re-erected and there is a sense of peace and prosperity.

Discussion Starters

1. Compare and contrast Ezekiel's description of the temple with that found in 1 Kings 6–8 of Solomon's temple, and the one in Revelation 11.

2. Look up 2 Chronicles 7 to discuss what happened when God's glory first filled Solomon's temple.

3. The temple was the way the people gained access to God, although it also kept out Gentiles and others could only go in so far. Why was this, and what barriers can we put up that stop us from getting near to God?

4. Ezekiel's vision of the temple was meant to lead the people into new, faith-filled, faithful behaviour. Keeping a vision of the cross in mind can help us to do the same. What can happen otherwise?

5. Look at the way Joshua divided the land up between the tribes (Josh. 15–19) and discuss the differences between that and what we read in Ezekiel.

_____

_____

_____

_____

6. Why was this description of the division of land so important?

_____

_____

_____

_____

7. Look up the other descriptions of the 'river of God' found in Revelation 22:1–2 and Genesis 2:10. What does the river symbolise?

_____

_____

_____

_____

8. Take some time to discuss what you feel you have gained from this study guide – perhaps you have gained knowledge of things that you didn't know previously, or challenges that you can continue to apply to your lives.

_____

_____

_____

_____

Personal Application

After reading the incredibly detailed description of the temple this week, it is mind-blowing to meditate on the fact that *we* are the temple that God inhabits now. As 1 Corinthians 3:16 reminds us: 'Don't you know that you yourselves are God's temple and that God's Spirit lives among you?' What a privilege – but this should also affect what we take into our bodies. For example, do you monitor what you watch, read and listen to? 1 Peter 2:9 tells us that we are also His royal priesthood: 'you are a chosen people, a royal priesthood, a holy nation, God's special possession, that you may declare the praises of him who called you out of darkness into his wonderful light.' How amazing!

Seeing Jesus in the Scriptures

A man that looked like bronze, and also called Ezekiel a 'son of man', showed him the vision we have looked at this week. He remained with Ezekiel throughout (transporting him to different aspects of the temple – such as in Ezekiel 43:1). This may well have been Jesus.

During His ministry, Jesus also had things to say about the temple and river. In His day, King Herod was in the laborious process of rebuilding the temple (somewhat as a status symbol). Jesus was not impressed though. In John 2, when Jesus cleared the temple of all those selling in it, He talked of how the temple would be destroyed (and rebuilt). He was talking about Himself here (see John 2:13–22), but interestingly Herod's temple had not been completed for long when it was pulled down by the Romans in AD 70.

As we end this study guide, let's remember that Jesus also likened believing in Him to a river: 'Whoever believes in me, as Scripture has said, rivers of living water will flow from within them' (John 7:38).

Leader's Notes

These leader's notes have been written to support you as you lead your small group through what I hope will be informative and life-giving discussions together.

Week One: Called and commissioned

Icebreaker

This is simply to get people talking and to prepare them for the subject, but hopefully the discussion will centre on how real a dream/vision can seem.

Discussion Starters

1. Sometimes we can miss out on a job opportunity, a promotion or get hurt by someone close to us – these are all disappointments that can cause bitterness to take root if we aren't careful. Then there can also be unexpected tragedies such as loss or illness. In these situations, do we, like the Israelites, begin to question whether God is there, or wonder if He no longer cares, or do we instead cling to what we know about Him even when we don't understand what is going on? Try to facilitate some honest discussion, but do be sensitive to any ongoing difficulties, which someone might be facing.

2. Here are some possible references you might want to use:
   - Isaiah 6:1: Isaiah received a vision of the throne of God 'high and lifted up', with His train filling the whole temple.

- 2 Chronicles 18:18: this vision of God on His throne was given purely to the prophet Micaiah. When the king of Judah, Zekekiah, was in an alliance with King Ahab, they asked prophets whether they would be victorious against Ramoth Gilead in war. The vision showed God's power and majesty – with multitudes surrounding Him. And yet the word from God was not a positive one – He would not protect them in battle. Only the obedient Micaiah saw the vision of God's throne.

- Psalm 11:4 talks of God seated on His throne observing everyone on earth – which reinforces the idea of the eyes we see in Ezekiel's vision of the throne.

- Daniel 7:9 depicts another striking vision that has a fiery throne.

- If you want to look at a New Testament example too, see Revelation 4.

3. Ezekiel's vision culminated in him seeing 'a figure like that of a man' (Ezek. 1:26). The description of a glowing, fiery, brilliant figure with a radiance all around Him has similarities to the one found in Revelation 1:12–18, in which we are told His eyes 'were like blazing fire' and His feet 'like bronze glowing in a furnace'. The glory of God that Ezekiel saw, which called him to be God's prophet, forewarned of God's judgment. The figure in Revelation is the one who now 'holds the keys of death and Hades' (Rev. 1:18). He is the one able to judge the world – as He has paid the ultimate sacrifice in order to save those who call on His name.

4. In Genesis 5:12–17, God indicates that the rainbow is a sign of His covenant with His people. Noah had just survived the flood in which God wiped out the rest of the world due to the people's wickedness. The rainbow was a promise that He would never do so again – a sign that even when His judgment came in the future He would remember mercy.

5. John's experience is very similar – although it is an angel who passes him the scroll, it is the voice of God that tells him to eat it. While it tasted sweet as honey, just as Ezekiel's had, it turned sour in his stomach – an indication that he too had a difficult prophesy to bring. You could discuss why you think Ezekiel didn't have the sour experience (pure conjecture, but may make an interesting discussion).

6. You could reference Isaiah 6 again here because Isaiah was totally overwhelmed by seeing God in His throne room (also John in Revelation 1:18 and Paul at his conversion in Acts 9).

7. The creatures were a combination of animals, humans and angels. This is symbolic of all the living beings that God has created. They also represent the three main orders. We are told they each had four faces (and wings): lion, ox, human and an eagle. Some believe they are the highest examples of creation, with the lion representing strength, the ox diligence, the human intelligence and the eagle divinity. The Early Church fathers also connected these four faces with the Gospels: the lion with Matthew (Jesus as the Lion of Judah), the ox with Mark (Christ the servant who took our yoke), the man with Luke (Jesus was the perfect human) and the eagle with John (Jesus the Son of God – divine).

8. Our 'post-truth' culture does not like the black-and-white aspect of the gospel. While we need to share with grace and humility, it is also important not to give up the mission Jesus gave us when those around us don't seem to respond well to the message.

Week Two: Visual representations of God's judgment

Icebreaker

Again, this is just to start people talking and thinking about how we usually try to persuade people with words – whereas God asked Ezekiel to show the people through some very odd actions!

Discussion Starters

1. The serpent in Genesis twisted God's words, saying 'Did God really say...'. As soon as that question enters our minds we are in dangerous territory. In 1 Samuel 13, King Saul knew that an offering needed to be made in order to enquire of God, but he did not wait for the prophet to arrive. Samuel was the one God had appointed to do this job, but Saul did it himself – and it cost him the kingship.

2. See Ezekiel 7–8: sacrificing to idols, immorality, exploiting the vulnerable, lying – basically having contempt for all of God's Commandments. They had allowed the surrounding cultures to influence them rather than staying pure.

3. Using human excrement would have violated God's own laws of purity (see Lev. 21–22, 23:12–14). This would have been a very visual representation of how defiled the people were, but for Ezekiel, who had trained as a priest, keeping the laws would have been a natural way of life.

4. In Egypt, God told the Israelites to mark their doors with the blood of a spotless lamb in order for the angel of death to pass over their houses when he visited, striking the firstborn of every Egyptian family (see Exod. 12:12–13). Revelation 7:3 talks about God marking the foreheads of all those who will be saved.

5. With God's heart set to judgment against the city of Sodom, Abraham pleaded before God as to whether He would save it if some righteous people were found there (see Gen. 18:16–33). You may want to talk around the subject of God's judgment and His mercy – why, for example, did He let Abraham question His justice?

6. Both the chief leaders of the city of Jerusalem, and the false prophets who were feeding the people lies, were influencing everyone. Their voices were the ones that people heard, and so, in effect, they were leading them astray. God holds those who are in a position of leadership accountable. They may have been saying what the people wanted to hear, so thereby seemingly providing a message of comfort, but, ultimately, they were doing the people harm. (Scriptures about the responsibility of leaders: Luke 12:48, Acts 20:28, Heb. 13:17, 1 Peter 5:1–4. In 2 Peter 2:19, Peter talks about false teachers and those they entice being enslaved by immorality.) We will learn more about how God feels about corrupt leaders in Ezekiel 34.

7. Creating a new heart can only be done by the Holy Spirit, but, as we open our hearts up and allow Him to change them, we will no longer be swayed by other things but will only long for our Father and God.

You may also want to mention Proverbs 4:23 here, and explain that, in Old Testament times, the heart was considered as the core of a person's intellect, will and spiritual being. Luke 12:34 reveals that what we treasure most has our heart. Do we treasure God above all?

8. Jesus rode from the Mount of Olives into Jerusalem, and from there He foretold how the New Testament temple would be destroyed (which happened in AD 70). He was also making reference to the fact that He would be killed (in Mark 14:58 and John 2:13–22 He revealed how He would rise again). Jesus taught on the Mount of Olives in Matthew 24–25, went there with His disciples before His arrest (Matt. 26:30) and also ascended into heaven from it (see Luke 24:50, Acts 1:9–12 – Bethany is on the south-eastern slope of the Mount of Olives). The Mount of Olives was also the place that the prophet Zechariah had said the Messiah would establish His kingdom from (Zech. 14:4).

Week Three: Parables and other stark messages

Icebreaker

This is to set up people to think about how much it must have cost Ezekiel to obey God's rather strange instructions at times. With people not listening to him, he must have felt extremely isolated. Also encourage people to think about the starkness of some of his messages – while we need to be mindful of our delivery when sharing what we feel God has given us to say, sometimes we can sugarcoat truth the point that we are actually diluting it.

Discussion Starters

1. Using the vine image was a traditional Hebrew way of describing what was usually the fruitfulness of a person or people group (see Gen. 49:22 for instance). As Jesus explained in Matthew 7:15–23, each of us should be bearing good fruit. If we are not, we will be pruned, or even cut off. You may want to bring in John 15, to expand the discussion to look at how Jesus is the true vine, God the gardener and we undergo pruning – there is a difference between cutting off and cutting back. In Ezekiel's parable there is no mention of fruit – it's almost as if things have gone past that; there is no life left even in the wood itself.

2. The language is incredibly vivid here. It is easy to imagine how vulnerable the child that had been abandoned was, and yet God cared for her. When she was old enough for marriage, Ezekiel 16:8 indicates that God became her bridegroom – He pledged His oath to her (that's what spreading the corner of the garment means – it's about protection, see Ruth 3:9). The language gets more and more graphic, sexual and violent in content. Ezekiel pulled no punches in exploring how degraded the people had become. It is like we can literally sense God's anger dripping from the words. (You may want to discuss how people feel about this portion of Scripture as it is quite disturbing to read, but that is precisely the point of it.)

3. Sodom became a symbol of corruption and God destroyed the whole city. And yet in our passage He talks not of their sexual sins (although He does mention 'detestable practices') but of pride, laziness, gluttony and arrogance. You may want to discuss how we tend to 'grade' sins and yet God doesn't.

4. There are so many parables in the Gospels that you can simply go with whatever people want to discuss. What is interesting is the parallels between Jesus and Ezekiel – how they both used parables to really bring home their messages (although, as Jesus Himself said in Mark 4:12, referencing Isaiah 6:9–10, parables can only be understood by those who really want to understand and many want to live in a state of ignorance). This goes back to God knowing the state of our hearts again. His message was for the few who would turn to Him, while He knew the majority wouldn't. Jesus always took the time to explain His parables to His disciples.

5. Ezekiel was telling people that the situation was far worse than they realised. They couldn't blame anyone else but themselves. And, on top of that, each one will stand before God alone to give an account of their lives (2 Cor. 5:10). The Bible says that 'all have sinned and fall short of the glory of God' (Rom. 3:23). Think back to the description of God on His throne; it is no wonder we fall short! The whole of Romans 3 gives a great explanation of our fallen state and the righteousness that Jesus gives us. However, even as we celebrate this message of grace, we need to consider the question that Paul asks in Romans 6:1, 'Shall we go on sinning?' He reminds us that we are dead to sin and therefore we are to be proactive in running from it (see vv11–14).

6.   The book of Lamentations is an obvious example
as it is full of lament! Written by Jeremiah, he is
lamenting over the state of the people and God's
judgment. Jesus Himself expressed lament over
Jerusalem in Matthew 23:37.

Habakkuk 3:17–18 is another example of lament.
In a time of difficulty, Habakkuk took his frustrations
to God, asking why and how long in the first chapter,
but settling in his heart to trust God by the third.
This is often the pattern found in the laments in the
psalms too (see, for example, Psa. 3; 13; 28; 142). The
psalms are great examples of using lament in worship
as so many of them were set to music. You may
want to discuss how effective you feel your church
is at providing space for lament in times of corporate
worship.

7.   Hosea was told to marry an unfaithful woman
– a prostitute – who kept going back to her old
ways. This was a practical illustration of Israel's
own unfaithfulness but how it must have pained
the prophet! Obeying God can often come with
a heavy price – and yet disobeying Him has an
even heavier one.

8.   Once the exiles heard about the destruction of
the temple (which happens in chapter 33), Ezekiel's
strange behaviour was vindicated! Everything that
he had said and done was proved to be true so the
people realised that he was indeed God's prophet.

Week Four: Surrounding nations

Icebreaker

This is to give people a sense of the geography and to
understand how Judah was surrounded by nations that
directly affected them. Pick out as many as you can from
the following: Ammon, Moab, Edom, Philistia, Tyre (capital
of Phoenicia), Egypt and Lebanon. (You may need to use
more than one map in order to find all the countries.)

Discussion Starters

1. Amos is speaking to the northern tribes, rather than
    the southern. He covers punishment – of both God's
    people but also the surrounding nations, but does
    it the other way round to Ezekiel. The people may
    well have been complacent, thinking that God was
    protecting them by punishing the other nations,
    and yet perhaps that makes the message even more
    powerful when he turns it onto them!

2. The main reasons for God's judgment against each
    neighbouring country are:
    • **Ammon:** gloating,
    • **Moab:** contempt for Judah and rejection of her
      being a set-apart nation,
    • **Edom:** non-specific but obviously some kind
      of spiteful revenge,
    • **Philista:** vengeful revenge,
    • **Tyre:** glee (and greed) at having the trade all
      for itself.

3. Psalm 137 includes a reflection on how difficult it
    is to sing about God in a foreign land, but then it
    finishes with a very destructive: 'Happy shall he
    be who dashes your little ones against the stones'
    (v9). This is actually making a direct reference back

to the way the Edomites treated them when they attacked Jerusalem – they took babies by the ankles and smashed their brains out against the walls of Jerusalem. This psalm was therefore indicating that they wanted the Edomites to understand what it feels like to suffer in the way they had.

4. Earthly kings lamented, and the local people mourned, the fall of both Tyre and Rome (in Revelation John refers to 'Babylon' – this is both an all-encompassing term for all the evil power in the world, as well as Rome). Both passages talk about how the two powers exploited others and became proud. Ultimately, God has set His face against them so they will be destroyed.

5. Daniel put his wisdom down to God (see Dan. 1–3, particularly 2:27–28). Truly wise people recognise that we are totally dependent on God for everything. You may want to look up 1 Corinthians 1:20–25 together to discuss this idea further – it talks about the foolishness of God being wiser than human wisdom.

6. Genesis 1 indicates that this 'serpent' or 'monster' was created – it was not a pre-creation opponent of God, which means it is not on His level. However Pharaoh was described like a mythological creature, who was crushing all those around him.

7. Egypt had taken great pride in its strength and beauty, as it had provided shelter (patronage) for many other nations over the years. The text even says that it was more beautiful than any tree in God's garden. And yet there is an indication that God allowed it to enjoy its great pride for a time, as He was setting it up for an even bigger downfall.

8. Our culture has the approach that whatever you believe to be true is fine for you. Many people also feel that it is fine for people to have their own religion, as there is more than one possible way to connect with a higher being. But in John 14:6, Jesus indicates that He is the only way. Of course we need to speak with grace, but we still need to remain clear about the truth.

Week Five: A renewal of God's promises

Icebreaker

The next few weeks are about God's promise of restoration, so this icebreaker is to get people thinking about waiting faithfully with anticipation for God to move.

Discussion Starters

1. Most of the Old Testament prophets spoke God's words of warning to the people. While they may have listened occasionally, the hallmark of much of what is recorded is the faithfulness of the one prophet – and the faithlessness of the people. For example, Jeremiah, a contemporary of Ezekiel, had 40 years of speaking God's message with nobody listening. In the New Testament, the majority of the religious leaders didn't listen to Jesus, and also paid no attention to the apostles after Him.

2. Bad shepherd: Good shepherd:

- Selfish, looked   • Looked after the flock,
  after self   often putting self in
                                danger to do so

- Concerned   • Sought out the
  with own health   weak, sick and lost

- Ruled harshly   • Cared for sheep
                                tenderly and lovingly

- Abandoned and   • Gathered and
  scattered sheep   protected sheep

3. Give plenty of time for quiet meditation but also
encourage people to bring whatever ideas they have
from that time. Some thoughts you may want to add
could be that God provides rest, security and someone
we can trust and follow.

4. You may want to discuss the use of imagery to depict
new life, but ultimately it was about God's restoration
and the rebuilding of the nation Israel.

5. Old covenant: New covenant:

- Written on   • Written on people's
  tablets of stone   hearts

- Based on following   • Based on a desire
  the law   to follow God

- Needed continual   • Based on Jesus'
  blood sacrifice   once-for-all sacrifice

- A legal relationship   • A love-based,
                                personal relationship

6. Lead some open discussion on this subject – there is no right or wrong answer here, but it would be interesting to talk about whether we honour prophets in our time or dismiss them too quickly. Do we take the time to weigh up what they say against the plumb line of the Bible?

7. It is interesting to note that both these chapters were being spoken to different groups of Israel at the same time. Even though both groups of people were in different places, they each tried to blame God's judgment on previous generations rather than taking responsibility for themselves. Both chapters also speak of restoration – which occurred in what was the near future for Israel, but also looking forward to when Jesus would come.

8. If God can restore Israel from the state of disobedience it was in, He can bring a church back to life. We can continue praying for renewal and restoration, reminding ourselves of this verse as we ask for more of His Spirit in our local churches.

Week Six: God's triumph over evil

Icebreaker

The chapters covered in Ezekiel this week can be quite confusing, so an overview of Israel's history – their unfaithfulness, God's use of surrounding nations to teach them to follow Him and ultimately His salvation – is useful. The reading from Romans will also provide an overview of Israel's past.

Discussion Starters

1. Some say that Ezekiel is prophesying about the end of time battle recorded in Revelation, while others point out there are too many differences between the two accounts (for example, in Revelation 20, Magog is a person associated with Gog, but in Ezekiel it is a place – but both talk about a group of countries rising up to destroy God's people, and He ultimately being victorious against them). Facilitate a discussion, to see what the group thinks.

2. Examples of what God is saying He will do against the nations can be found in Ezekiel 38:4,21–23; 39:2–6. How He will restore His people is shown in Ezekiel 39:25–29 and His holiness features in Ezekiel 38:23; 39:7,21–28.

3. The forces of evil are sometimes described as coming from 'the north'. The language is most similar to the way Jeremiah spoke God's prophecies to the people – for an example see Jeremiah 4:5–6:26. You could also look at Joel 2:28–32, Amos 5:18–20, Zephaniah 1:14–18, Isaiah 29:5–8; 66:15 and Zechariah 12:1–9; 14:1–15.

4. Human nature seems to always look elsewhere with a 'grass is greener' mindset. For example, when God brought the people out of captivity in Egypt, it wasn't long before they were bored of manna and living in tents, and longed for the comforts of Egypt (see Num. 11). However, when we are 'squeezed' by difficulties our hearts are turned towards God as we remember His character and His promises to rescue us.

5. While God may not always intervene in our difficulties and alleviate them all straightaway, we can rest assured that the whole of history is in His hands and one day He will have the final victory over all forces of evil. We may not understand why He doesn't change circumstances right now, but He sees a much fuller picture than we do.

6. Ezekiel never shied away from proclaiming God's full message, no matter how harsh the language. Here God's judgment is being poured out against those who have committed horrendous acts. The idea of feasting could indicate a joy in being victorious over those who have oppressed for so long, or it may just be corresponding imagery of a similar weight to their enemies' atrocities against them.

7. It is so important that God's name continues to be glorified and we can still do that in the midst of suffering. In Acts 7:54–60, Stephen stayed strong even when he was being stoned, his face firmly fixed on Jesus in heaven as he was dying. Once full of the Holy Spirit, the apostles each stood firm in the face of persecution (it is interesting to compare this to how full of fear they were beforehand – such as when Jesus was arrested). Obviously, Jesus on the cross is the ultimate example of glorifying God, even during persecution.

8. You may want to look up some websites such as www.opendoorsuk.org to find some specifics. Take some time to pray for the Church around the world – for God's strengthening, protection and, ultimately, that His name will be proclaimed in every nation on earth.

Week Seven: A vision of restoration

Icebreaker

The aim this week is to get people thinking about the process of restoration. It takes time and effort but is ultimately for the purpose of creating something more beautiful – which is what God does with us.

Discussion Starters

1. The temple in Ezekiel was a lot larger than Solomon's temple, had no holy of holies and no ark of the covenant. However, both were extremely opulent. The description of the temple in Revelation is quite short – some believe it is not a literal temple but refers to God's people who are being measured in order to be protected by God (see Rev. 11:1).

2. God's glory came down, consumed the offering and was so overpowering that the priests could not enter the temple. The people's response was to worship, which was what Ezekiel did, even though he was allowed to see God's glory for himself (see Ezek. 43:1–5).

3. All the rules that God put in place regarding access to the temple were to act as a reminder of the barrier of sin and the need for that sin to be atoned for. In a similar way, our sin can stop us from drawing close to God if we do not confess it (1 John 1:9). But we have a promise that God *will* forgive us if we repent, and we are already cleansed and made pure in Christ (see Heb. 10:19–22). This means that we no longer need to be fearful of not being clean enough to enter His presence.

4. Without a clear vision of the cross, we can either fall into legalism, in which we think we should be earning our salvation, or we become too lax in our approach to sin, forgetting how serious it is. So serious that it meant Jesus had to come in human form and take on the sin of all humanity. That is definitely sobering and worth reflecting on regularly lest we begin to take it for granted.

5. In Ezekiel the land was simply allocated in horizontal strips from east to west, while Joshua's allocation was very complicated and time consuming (and took up many more chapters!). In Ezekiel, it was not done via the order of birth, and there are indications that perhaps it is not to be read literally as there is a spiritual message within it. For example, the tribe of Dan, which was provided for last in the first division of Canaan (see Josh. 19:40), was first provided for here. This reflects the teaching that the last shall be first and vice versa (see Matt. 19:30).

6. Even though there is less space given over to the division of land in Ezekiel as there was in Joshua, it can still seem quite a tedious portion of text to our modern eyes. However, to the displaced Israelites, land was so important. They hadn't had a place to call their own during the time they were in exile. Their land was their livelihood but also gave them their identity. Being given land by God showed them that they were accepted, that they belonged.

7. The river symbolises God's life and healing. It flows directly from the throne of God and the Lamb, who was the one whose sacrifice brought the life-source into being for us all.

8. Give space for everyone who wants to answer. You might like to then pray for one another before finishing this final session.

Notes…

Latest Resources

The Popular *Cover to Cover* Bible Study Series

1 Corinthians
Growing a Spirit-filled church
ISBN: 978-1-85345-374-8

2 Corinthians
Restoring harmony
ISBN: 978-1-85345-551-3

1,2,3 John
Walking in the truth
ISBN: 978-1-78259-763-6

1 Peter
Good reasons for hope
ISBN: 978-1-78259-088-0

2 Peter
Living in the light of God's promises
ISBN: 978-1-78259-403-1

23rd Psalm
The Lord is my shepherd
ISBN: 978-1-85345-449-3

1 Timothy
Healthy churches –
effective Christians
ISBN: 978-1-85345-291-8

2 Timothy and Titus
Vital Christianity
ISBN: 978-1-85345-338-0

Abraham
Adventures of faith
ISBN: 978-1-78259-089-7

Acts 1-12
Church on the move
ISBN: 978-1-85345-574-2

Acts 13-28
To the ends of the earth
ISBN: 978-1-85345-592-6

Barnabas
Son of encouragement
ISBN: 978-1-85345-911-5

Bible Genres
Hearing what the Bible really says
ISBN: 978-1-85345-987-0

Daniel
Living boldly for God
ISBN: 978-1-85345-986-3

David
A man after God's own heart
ISBN: 978-1-78259-444-4

Ecclesiastes
Hard questions and
spiritual answers
ISBN: 978-1-85345-371-7

Elijah
A man and his God
ISBN: 978-1-85345-575-9

Elisha
A lesson in faithfulness
ISBN: 978-1-78259-494-9

Ephesians
Claiming your inheritance
ISBN: 978-1-85345-229-1

Esther
For such a time as this
ISBN: 978-1-85345-511-7

Ezekiel
A prophet for all times
ISBN: 978-1-78259-836-7

Fruit of the Spirit
Growing more like Jesus
ISBN: 978-1-85345-375-5

Galatians
Freedom in Christ
ISBN: 978-1-85345-648-0

God's Rescue Plan
Finding God's fingerprints
on human history
ISBN: 978-1-85345-294-9

Great Prayers of the Bible
Applying them to our lives today
ISBN: 978-1-85345-253-6

Habakkuk
Choosing God's way
ISBN: 978-1-78259-843-5

Haggai
Motivating God's people
ISBN: 978-1-78259-686-8

Hebrews
Jesus – simply the best
ISBN: 978-1-85345-337-3

Hosea
The love that never fails
ISBN: 978-1-85345-290-1

Isaiah 1-39
Prophet to the nations
ISBN: 978-1-85345-510-0

Isaiah 40–66
Prophet of restoration
ISBN: 978-1-85345-550-6

Jacob
Taking hold of God's blessing
ISBN: 978-1-78259-685-1

James
Faith in action
ISBN: 978-1-85345-293-2

Jeremiah
The passionate prophet
ISBN: 978-1-85345-372-4

John's Gospel
Exploring the seven miraculous signs
ISBN: 978-1-85345-295-6

Jonah
Rescued from the depths
ISBN: 978-1-78259-762-9

Joseph
The power of forgiveness and reconciliation
ISBN: 978-1-85345-252-9

Joshua 1–10
Hand in hand with God
ISBN: 978-1-85345-542-7

Judges 1–8
The spiral of faith
ISBN: 978-1-85345-681-7

Judges 9–21
Learning to live God's way
ISBN: 978-1-85345-910-8

Luke
A prescription for living
ISBN: 978-1-78259-270-9

Mark
Life as it is meant to be lived
ISBN: 978-1-85345-233-8

Mary
The mother of Jesus
ISBN: 978-1-78259-402-4

Moses
Face to face with God
ISBN: 978-1-85345-336-6

Names of God
Exploring the depths of God's character
ISBN: 978-1-85345-680-0

Nehemiah
Principles for life
ISBN: 978-1-85345-335-9

Parables
Communicating God on earth
ISBN: 978-1-85345-340-3

Philemon
From slavery to freedom
ISBN: 978-1-85345-453-0

Philippians
Living for the sake of the gospel
ISBN: 978-1-85345-421-9

Prayers of Jesus
Hearing His heartbeat
ISBN: 978-1-85345-647-3

Proverbs
Living a life of wisdom
ISBN: 978-1-85345-373-1

Revelation 1–3
Christ's call to the Church
ISBN: 978-1-85345-461-5

Revelation 4–22
The Lamb wins! Christ's final victory
ISBN: 978-1-85345-411-0

Rivers of Justice
Responding to God's call to righteousness today
ISBN: 978-1-85345-339-7

Ruth
Loving kindness in action
ISBN: 978-1-85345-231-4

The Armour of God
Living in His strength
ISBN: 978-1-78259-583-0

The Beatitudes
Immersed in the grace of Christ
ISBN: 978-1-78259-495-6

The Covenants
God's promises and their relevance today
ISBN: 978-1-85345-255-0

The Creed
Belief in action
ISBN: 978-1-78259-202-0

The Divine Blueprint
God's extraordinary power in ordinary lives
ISBN: 978-1-85345-292-5

The Holy Spirit
Understanding and experiencing Him
ISBN: 978-1-85345-254-3

The Image of God
His attributes and character
ISBN: 978-1-85345-228-4

The Kingdom
Studies from Matthew's Gospel
ISBN: 978-1-85345-251-2

The Letter to the Colossians
In Christ alone
ISBN: 978-1-855345-405-9

The Letter to the Romans
Good news for everyone
ISBN: 978-1-85345-250-5

The Lord's Prayer
Praying Jesus' way
ISBN: 978-1-85345-460-8

The Prodigal Son
Amazing grace
ISBN: 978-1-85345-412-7

The Second Coming
Living in the light of Jesus' return
ISBN: 978-1-85345-422-6

The Sermon on the Mount
Life within the new covenant
ISBN: 978-1-85345-370-0

Thessalonians
Building Church in changing times
ISBN: 978-1-78259-443-7

The Ten Commandments
Living God's Way
ISBN: 978-1-85345-593-3

The Uniqueness of our Faith
What makes Christianity distinctive?
ISBN: 978-1-85345-232-1

For current prices or to order, visit **www.cwr.org.uk/shop**
Available online or from Christian bookshops.

Be inspired by God.
Every day.

Confidently face life's challenges by equipping yourself daily with God's Word. There is something for everyone...

Every Day with Jesus

Selwyn Hughes' renowned writing is updated by Mick Brooks into these trusted and popular notes.

Life Every Day

Jeff Lucas helps apply the Bible to daily life through his trademark humour and insight.

Inspiring Women
Every Day

Encouragement, uplifting scriptures and insightful daily thoughts for women.

The Manual

Straight-talking guide to help men walk daily with God. Written by Carl Beech.

To find out more about all our daily Bible reading notes, or to take out a subscription, visit **www.cwr.org.uk/biblenotes** or call 01252 784700.
Also available in Christian bookshops.

 Printed format Large print format  Email format Ebook format

SmallGroup central

All of our small group ideas and resources in one place

Online:

www.smallgroupcentral.org.uk
is filled with free video teaching, tools, articles and a whole host of ideas.

On the road:

A range of seminars themed for small groups can be brought to your local community. Contact us at ***hello@smallgroupcentral.org.uk***

In print:

Books, study guides and DVDs covering an extensive list of themes, Bible books and life issues.

Find out more at:
www.smallgroupcentral.org.uk

Courses and events

Waverley Abbey College

Publishing and media

Conference facilities

Transforming lives

CWR's vision is to enable people to experience personal transformation through applying God's Word to their lives and relationships.

Our Bible-based training and resources help people around the world to:
• Grow in their walk with God
• Understand and apply Scripture to their lives
• Resource themselves and their church
• Develop pastoral care and counselling skills
• Train for leadership
• Strengthen relationships, marriage and family life and much more.

Our insightful writers provide daily Bible reading notes and other resources for all ages, and our experienced course designers and presenters have gained an international reputation for excellence and effectiveness.

CWR's Training and Conference Centre in Surrey, England, provides excellent facilities in an idyllic setting – ideal for both learning and spiritual refreshment.

CWR Applying God's Word
to everyday life and relationships

CWR, Waverley Abbey House,
Waverley Lane, Farnham,
Surrey GU9 8EP, UK

Telephone: **+44 (0)1252 784700**
Email: **info@cwr.org.uk**
Website: **www.cwr.org.uk**

Registered Charity No. 294387
Company Registration No. 1990308